A LITTLE CAMEL FOR BABY JESUS

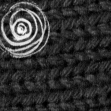

A LITTLE CAMEL FOR BABY JESUS

Written and Illustrated by

Maria Gianola

Pauline
BOOKS & MEDIA
Boston

Library of Congress Control Number: 2019937413
CIP data is available.

ISBN-10: 0-8198- 4601-5
ISBN-13: 978-0-8198- 4601-3

Translated by Marlyn Evangelina Monge, FSP

Originally published in Italian as *Un piccolo cammello per Gesù*, written and illustrated by Maria Gianola © Editrice Elledici, in person of the legal representative don Mauro Balma with registered office in Castelnuovo don Bosco (AT) — Fraz. Morialdo, 30 and headquarter in Torino — Corso Francia, 333/3 Italia. P.IVA/C.F. 00070920053.

Published by Pauline Books & Media, 50 Saint Pauls Avenue, Boston, MA 02130-3491

Printed in the U.S.A.

ALCFBJ VSAUSAPEOILL3-2510149 4601-5

www.pauline.org

Pauline Books & Media is the publishing house of the Daughters of St. Paul, an international congregation of women religious serving the Church with the communications media.

1 2 3 4 5 6 7 8 9   23 22 21 20 19

"Whatever you did
for one of these least brothers and sisters
of mine, you did for me."

—Jesus

(Mt 25:40)

"The star we have been waiting for has appeared! A new king has been born!" announced the king one night.

"We will leave tomorrow
at sunset to follow the star!"

Joel was seven years old. He was the son of the king's stableman.

He helped his father care for the horses, the camels, the sheep, and the goats.

Knowing that it would be a long journey, Joel had helped his father to prepare everything: the blankets, the water, and the hay. The animals were ready.

The king's caravan traveled west.
Soon they met caravans from nearby kingdoms
and they all traveled together.

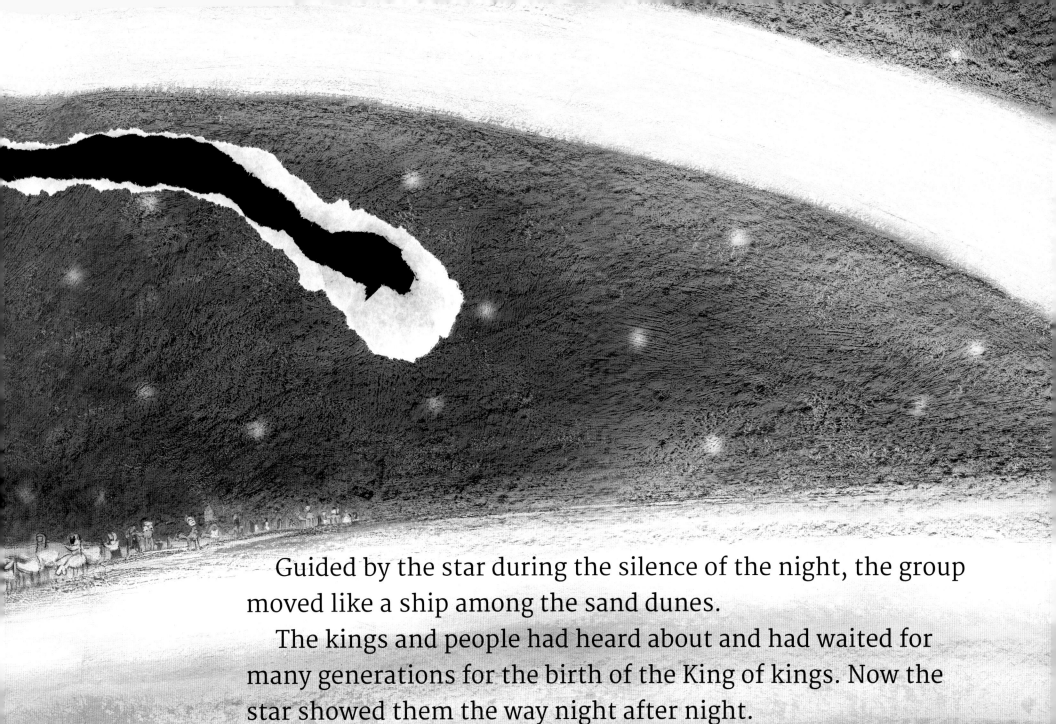

Guided by the star during the silence of the night, the group moved like a ship among the sand dunes.

The kings and people had heard about and had waited for many generations for the birth of the King of kings. Now the star showed them the way night after night.

My king has brought a gift of gold. The other kings are carrying incense and myrrh, thought Joel. *How can I meet this new King with empty hands?* he worried.

Then he had an idea. "I know how to whittle wood," he said. "I will bring the newborn King a little camel I can make with my own hands!"

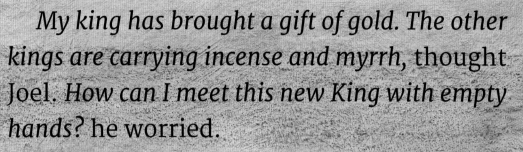

Joel worked on his gift at night while he rode his camel. When morning came and the caravan stopped to rest, Joel worked on his gift until he felt tired.

For many nights the caravan followed the star across mountains and deserts. Finally, they arrived outside a little town called Bethlehem. There the star stopped.

This must be where we
will meet the King of kings,
thought Joel.

17

The bright star in the sky lit the warm night. Although Joel was tired, he could not sleep. Then the quiet night was interrupted by a baby crying and crying. Joel could hear the baby's mother tirelessly singing a sweet lullaby.

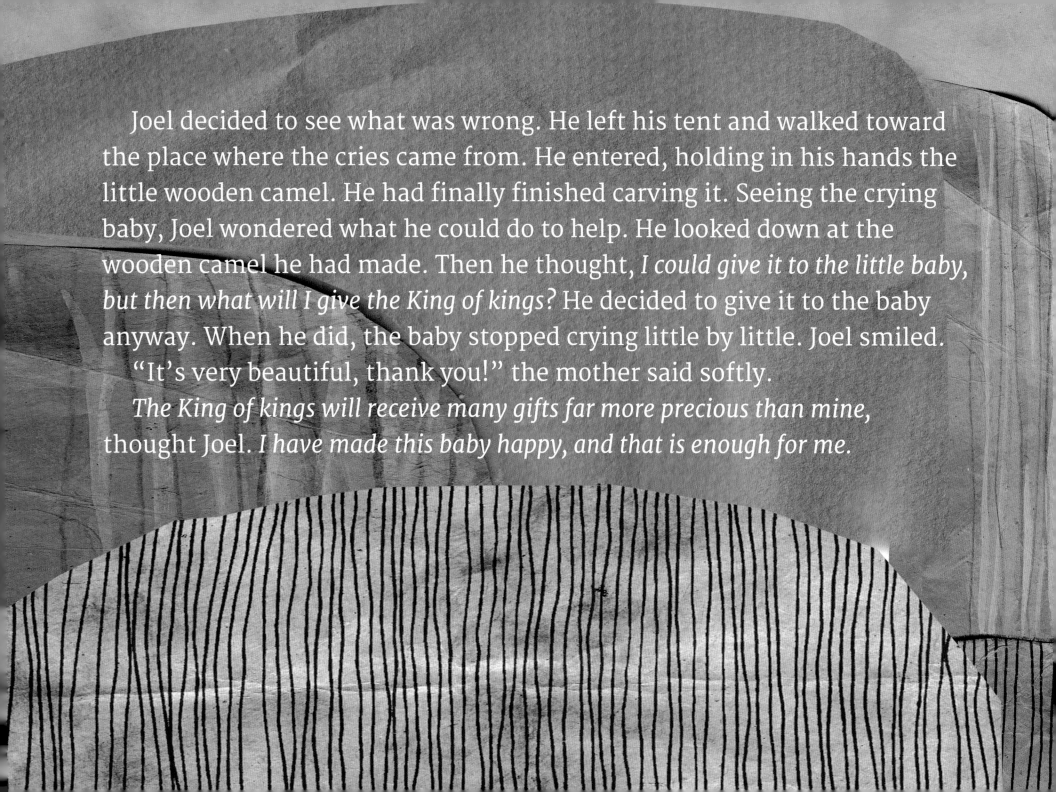

Joel decided to see what was wrong. He left his tent and walked toward the place where the cries came from. He entered, holding in his hands the little wooden camel. He had finally finished carving it. Seeing the crying baby, Joel wondered what he could do to help. He looked down at the wooden camel he had made. Then he thought, *I could give it to the little baby, but then what will I give the King of kings?* He decided to give it to the baby anyway. When he did, the baby stopped crying little by little. Joel smiled.

"It's very beautiful, thank you!" the mother said softly.

The King of kings will receive many gifts far more precious than mine, thought Joel. *I have made this baby happy, and that is enough for me.*

The next night the kings followed the star into Bethlehem. There they found the Lord, the awaited King of kings.

They knelt before him in adoration. They placed their gifts of gold, frankincense, and myrrh at the baby's feet.

Joel gasped when he saw the baby King of kings. Baby Jesus recognized little Joel among the important men. Jesus reached out for Joel, looked directly into his eyes, and gave him a great big smile.

Joel smiled back. Then Joel noticed what Jesus was holding tightly in his little hands. It was the camel he had carved—which, among all the gifts, was truly the most precious one.

23

Editor's Note

You can be like Joel, too! In fact, Jesus tells us he *wants* us to do what Joel did. Joel thought he gave his little camel to someone unimportant. Then, he learned that he actually gave his gift to the King of kings!

When Jesus was an adult, he told his friends, "Whatever you did for one of these least brothers and sisters of mine, you did for me." This means that when you do anything mean to anyone, you are doing it to Jesus! If you make fun of someone, you are making fun of Jesus. If you steal another person's candy, you are stealing from Jesus. If you hit someone, you are hitting Jesus.

But more importantly, this also means that when you do something nice for someone else, you are doing it for Jesus! When you help someone who has fallen down, you are helping Jesus. When you share a piece of candy or some of your lunch with another person, you are sharing with Jesus. Even when you donate some toys for children who do not have much, you are giving them to Jesus.

So when we meet people, it is good to treat them as if we are meeting the King of kings, who is Jesus.

What three things can you do today for someone else?

smile

God loves you

Tales and Legends from

Pauline kids

The 3 Trees
Adapted by Gabriel Ringlet
Illustrated by Daniella Oh

The Little Lost Lamb
Written and Illustrated by Geri Berger Haines

the Queen & the Cross
The Story of Saint Helen
Written by Cornelia Mary Bilinsky
Illustrated by Rebecca Stuhff

The Saint Who Fought the Dragon
The Story of Saint George
Written by Cornelia Mary Bilinsky
Illustrated by Theresa Fitzgerald

SANTA'S Secret Story
Written by Cornelia Mary Bilinsky
Illustrated by Candace Camling

Who are the Daughters of St. Paul?

We are Catholic sisters. Our mission is to be like Saint Paul and tell everyone about Jesus! There are so many ways for people to communicate with each other. We want to use all of them so everyone will know how much God loves us. We do this by printing books (you're holding one!), making radio shows, singing, helping people at our bookstores, using the internet, and in many other ways.

VISIT US AT WWW.PAULINE.ORG

Pauline
BOOKS & MEDIA

The Daughters of St. Paul operate book and media centers at the following addresses.
Visit, call, or write the one nearest you today, or find us at www.paulinestore.org.

CALIFORNIA
3908 Sepulveda Blvd, Culver City, CA 90230   310-397-8676
3250 Middlefield Road, Menlo Park, CA 94025   650-562-7060

FLORIDA
145 S.W. 107th Avenue, Miami, FL 33174   305-559-6715

HAWAII
1143 Bishop Street, Honolulu, HI 96813   808-521-2731

ILLINOIS
172 North Michigan Avenue, Chicago, IL 60601   312-346-4228

LOUISIANA
4403 Veterans Memorial Blvd, Metairie, LA 70006   504-887-7631

MASSACHUSETTS
885 Providence Hwy, Dedham, MA 02026   781-326-5385

MISSOURI
9804 Watson Road, St. Louis, MO 63126   314-965-3512

NEW YORK
115 E. 29th Street, New York City, NY 10016   212-754-1110

TEXAS
No book center; for parish exhibits or outreach evangelization, contact:
210-569-0500, or SanAntonio@paulinemedia.com, or P.O. Box 761416,
San Antonio, TX 78245

SOUTH CAROLINA
243 King Street, Charleston, SC 29401   843-577-0175

VIRGINIA
1025 King Street, Alexandria, VA 22314   703-549-3806

CANADA
3022 Dufferin Street, Toronto, Ontario, Canada M6B 3T5   416-781-9131

¡También somos su fuente para libros,
videos y música en español!

Smile
God loves you